The second 50 *Hobart Papers* will continue their characteristic approach to subjects insufficiently examined by economists: the analysis of the optimum use of scarce resources in response to consumer preferences within a legal and institutional framework governing the disposition of property, the conduct of contract and the means of exchange in the market-place.

Several *Hobart Papers* in the first 50 discussed the conditions of supply and demand of commodities or services not in themselves of large quantitative importance and perhaps therefore not commonly subjected to economic analysis but capable of illuminating fundamental principles and elements of policy. Among them were television, libraries, telephones and blood. Air transport for civilian passengers has developed rapidly since the end of the war as a result of an increase in demand resting on rising incomes and changing conditions of supply caused by scientific development. But it also operates in a framework of legal and other agreements which decide not only air fares but also the conditions of travel, the consequences of which have not received much attention from economists so that public debate and government policy has been formed, until recently, with too little assistance from economic analysis. The Institute accordingly invited two economists, Mr Michael Cooper and Mr Alan Maynard, from the University of Exeter to examine the economic implications of the legal and institutional framework within changing market conditions of supply and demand.

They have emerged with a well-researched and brightly written analysis and a confident series of conclusions. They present in an easily assimilable form much material on costs and fares for airlines over the world, the operation of the International Air Transport Association (IATA), the growth of air transport outside IATA, the structure and extent of competition between the airlines operating within IATA and outside it, the efforts to restrict competition and its consequences in new forms of competition that escape the internationally agreed rules by charter flights and affinity groups.

It would seem that the maintenance of safety in the air, and on the ground, has been made the reason or the pretext for restrictions on competition by limiting the entry of new competitors and the conditions on which they may compete. The error would thus appear to be a parallel to the *non sequitur* in the argument that to maintain standards in public houses or road transport it was necessary to restrict by licensing the numbers and the conduct of suppliers admitted. The economist's argument, to which there has so far been no convincing reply, is that the assurance of safety requires not restriction on numbers but the maintenance of standards.

It may be that recent British governments have shown themselves aware of the defects of the restriction of competition by IATA, and that technical advance and rising demand for air travel from middle- and low-income passengers will impel some airlines to offer cheaper air travel than is permitted within the IATA rules. But governments are normally conservative in maintaining outworn institutions and they are not known for alacrity in adapting them to new conditions. It is here that the Cooper/Maynard *Hobart Paper* may assist in clearing cobwebs from fusty minds and in accelerating reform by stimulating academic, public and political debate.

It would seem also that the people who pay the air fares, the consumers of air transport, are at long last organising themselves sufficiently to ask the Economic and Social Council of the United Nations to examine the IATA 'monopoly'. It would be a sad reflection on the working of parliamentary democracy, and of the claim of nationalised enterprises to serve the customer, if governments showed themselves more sensitive to the convenience of the suppliers than to the interests of consumers, and waited for the consumers to organise pressure groups before taking action.

The Institute is grateful to Mr G. J. Ponsonby, Mr Edwin J. Feulner Jr., author of *The Determination of International Air Fares*, of Washington, Dr Colin Clark, and other economists who wish to remain anonymous, for reading an early draft of the Paper and offering comments which the authors have borne in mind in their final revisions. The constitution of the Institute requires its Trustees, Directors and Advisers to dissociate themselves from authors' analysis and conclusions, but it offers Messrs Cooper and Maynard's *Paper* to students and teachers of economics, to the consumers of air transport, to politicians who have largely controlled and confined its development, and

[4]

perhaps to businessmen who might extend it to suit the potentially growing market more rapidly, as a study of an industry still in its youth that could benefit from working in a freer and more competitive market.

May 1971   EDITOR

THE AUTHORS

MICHAEL H. COOPER graduated from the University of Leicester in 1961. He undertook post-graduate research into the National Health Service at the University of Keele for two years; subsequently appointed Assistant Lecturer. Currently a Lecturer in Economics at the University of Exeter. He specialises in the social services; over 30 papers published in Italy, India, the United States and Britain.

Author of *Prices and Profits in the Pharmaceutical Industry* (Pergamon Press, Oxford, 1966); with A. J. Culyer, *The Price of Blood* (Hobart Paper 41, Institute of Economic Affairs, London, 1968); 'An Economic Analysis of Some Aspects of the National Health Service', in *Health Services Financing* (British Medical Association, London, 1970); and, with R. D. King, 'Sociological and Economic Problems of Prisoners' Work', in *Sociological Studies in the British Penal Services* (ed. Paul Halmos, Keele, 1965). Editor, Journal of *Social and Economic Administration*, since its inception in 1967, and of a series of occasional papers. Completing a textbook on health economics with A. J. Culyer.

ALAN K. MAYNARD was born in December 1944, and was educated at Calday Grange Grammar School, West Kirby, Cheshire, and the University of Newcastle-upon-Tyne, graduating B.A. (Economic Studies) with First Class Honours in 1967. From Newcastle he went to the University of York and graduated B.Phil. (Economics) in 1968. Since 1968 he has been a Lecturer in Economics at the University of Exeter.

He has just completed (with D. N. King) a study of the economic aspects of local government for the Hobart Papers; he specialises in the social services, the labour market and civil aviation.

AUTHORS' NOTE

Both authors are members of the *Zurich European Consumer Committee on Civil Aviation*. They should like to record their gratitude to its members for much discussion, debate and guidance over the past twelve months. In particular they should like to express their thanks to A. J. Lucking and to the Group's Hon. Secretary, George W. Smith. This *Paper* is solely the responsibility of the authors and in no way necessarily reflects the views of the Zurich Committee.

March 1971

M.H.C.

A.K.M.

CONTENTS

I. INTRODUCTION

Civil aviation is a young and rapidly growing industry. People use it and are affected by it both individually and collectively in a complex of ways. It can represent a business expense, a means to pleasure, national prestige or simply a noise overhead. Only a small minority have personal experience of it but all are aware of it. Most fear it.

Growth potential of air travel

Since 1948 the industry, as measured by passenger-kilometres flown, has grown 15-fold at an average annual rate of 14 per cent. Nevertheless in 1968 only 130 million passenger round-trips were made. Indeed only 27 million passengers embarked upon an international return flight, over 2½ million of which crossed the North Atlantic. The growth potential then remains largely untouched. How is it to be reached? Are we currently on the right lines? This *Paper* examines the economic implications of the present structure of international passenger air travel for the consumer.

We endorse at the outset the words of the Edwards Committee:

'One of the odd things about statements on civil air transport is that they very rarely talk about the customer in simple language. So let us say that in our view the primary long-term objective of a national policy towards commercial flying should be to see that each customer, be it for personal travel or freight, gets what he wants—not what somebody else thinks he ought to want—at the minimum economic price that can be contrived. Romantic, exciting and important though the airline business may be, it is, in the last analysis, there to do the same job as butchers, bakers or candlestick makers, i.e. to provide services for money. Many other objectives are talked about in connection with air transport, but we put this humdrum one right at the top. Moreover we believe that if any other objective conflicts with it the onus of justification should fall on those who want to press that objective against the interests of the consumer'.[1]

[1] 'The Edwards Committee Report', *The UK Committee of Enquiry into Civil Air Transport*, paras. 46 and 47, Cmnd. 4018, HMSO, 1969.

The two main bodies governing the industry, namely the International Civil Aviation Organisation (ICAO) and the International Air Transport Association (IATA) evolved, one directly, the other indirectly, from a Chicago meeting of government and airline representatives of 50 nations in 1944. The USA proposed a multilateral convention to establish complete freedom of the air. Its economic superiority plus a stock of heavy bombers and transports gave it a potential far above most other nations. The proposal ran counter to the spirit and letter of the Paris Conference of 1919 which gave nations sovereignty over their airspace for reasons of national security. The proposal, endorsed by Sweden and Holland, came to grief because the UK believed that there should be 'order in the air'.[1] In the event the only firm outcome of the meeting was the establishment of the ICAO as the 'central organisation for co-ordination' in the industry.[2] In practice the organisation (now part of the UN) has been a toothless bulldog resisting all efforts by member governments to discuss tariff issues.[3]

Whilst the governments of the world agreed to disagree, the representatives of airlines agreed to agree and IATA was born out of the ashes of their pre-war association. The airline chiefs were grateful that they had managed to create a simple cartel without undue government control. The price-cutting wars of the 1930s were now a thing of the past.

In the absence of a Chicago agreement a compromise was reached between the US and the UK in Bermuda in 1946. This compromise has since served as a model for many bilateral agreements between other governments since the war. Essentially it marked a withdrawal by the US. Fares were to be left to airlines to settle within IATA subject only to a veto by the governments concerned. The UK for its part agreed to a slightly more flexible arrangement than the strict regulations of capacity and the maintenance of 'order' it had formerly insisted upon. The two countries exchanged traffic rights between certain agreed city pairings and each party was allowed to license airlines to provide services on each route.

[1] K. G. J. Pillai, *The Air Net*, Grossman Publishers, New York, 1969, p. 85.
[2] M. R. Straszheim, *The International Airline Industry*, Brookings Institution, Washington, DC, 1969, p. 32.
[3] See Pillai, *op. cit.*, Ch. 8.

TABLE 1
SCHEDULED PASSENGER TRAFFIC, 1948–68

	Passengers Carried (millions)				
	1948	*1953*	*1958*	*1963*	*1968*
World Total	24	53	88	135	263
International Total	4	9	18	31	55
Domestic Total	20	44	70	104	208
North Atlantic—IATA	0.240	0.509	1.193	2.422	5.258
	Passenger Kilometres (millions)				
World	21,000	46,000	85,000	147,000	308,000
International	8,000	14,000	30,000	57,000	114,000
Domestic	13,000	32,000	55,000	90,000	194,000
North Atlantic—IATA	1,323	2,786	6,563	13,322	28,919

Source: IATA, *World Air Transport Statistics* (annual).

'Five freedoms of the air'

The Bermuda Agreement is often discussed in terms of the 'five freedoms of the air'. Assuming three countries, A, B and C and one airline owned by country A, the freedoms are as follows:

1. The right of A's airline to fly over B to get to C.

$$A \xrightarrow[B]{} C$$

2. The right of A's airline to land in B for fuel or maintenance but not to pick up or put down traffic.

$$\xrightarrow[A \quad B \quad C]{}$$

3. The right to set down traffic from A in B.
$$A \longrightarrow B$$
4. The right to carry traffic back to A from B.
$$A \longleftarrow B$$
5. The right of A's airline to collect traffic in B and fly them to C.

$$A \longrightarrow B \longrightarrow C$$

The Chicago Conference had discussed and agreed to freedoms 1 and 2. Bermuda was concerned with freedoms 3, 4

[12]

(TABLE 1 *continued*)

Comparison with Base Year 1948 = 1				Average Annual Growth Rate 1948/68 1953/68 1958/68 1963/68 per cent			
1953	1958	1963	1968	1948/68	1953/68	1958/68	1963/68
2.21	3.67	5.63	10.96	12.7	11.3	11.6	14.3
2.25	4.50	7.75	13.75	14.0	12.9	11.8	12.2
2.20	3.50	5.20	10.40	12.4	10.9	11.5	14.9
2.12	4.97	10.09	21.91	16.7	16.9	16.0	16.8
2.19	4.05	7.00	14.67	14.4	13.5	13.7	15.9
1.75	3.75	7.13	14.25	14.2	15.0	14.3	14.9
2.46	4.23	6.92	14.92	14.5	12.8	13.4	16.6
2.11	4.96	10.07	21.86	16.7	16.9	16.0	16.8

and 5, but in the main the outcome was ambiguous. According to this agreement the main point of services was to serve freedoms 3 and 4. That being so, there was to be no limit to capacity or to the picking up of incidental traffic whilst passing through (freedom 5) intermediate points. However, the agreement was so imprecise that it has led to many subsequent disputes, most of which have been settled in a restrictive manner to the cost of the fifth freedom. The Bermuda agreement's clause that account should be taken of 'local and regional services' has been used as a justification for such restrictions.

Subsequent bilateral agreements (without which entry by a commercial aircraft is illegal) have varied from a copy of the Bermuda agreement to extremely precise and rigorous capacity controls. Some cite cities whilst others are content to make general route descriptions.

In 1947 freedom of the air was only narrowly defeated in Geneva, but since then the system of bilateral agreements between nations agreeing on the market environment and of airlines agreeing on their fare structures within IATA has continued virtually unchallenged. A typical recent agreement is that between the UK and Algeria for services between Algiers and London. Each country is enabled to license one carrier. The agreement states that 'in operating the agreed services the airlines of each Contracting Party shall take into account the interests of the airlines of the other Contracting Party so as not to affect unduly the services which the latter provide on the whole or part of the same routes'.

Services should be consistent with 'reasonable load factors' and 'tariffs at reasonable levels' should be agreed by the two airlines through the auspices of IATA.[1]

Sometimes as a direct consequence of the inter-governmental level bilateral agreement, airlines have agreed to pool capacity and revenue in what amounts to a jointly-operated route. It is claimed that this complete removal of any competitive element yields the consumer a better service in controlled scheduling, rationalised use of capacity and economies of scale. In practice this pooling is a way of protecting small national airlines of under-developed countries and yet allowing the large lines to extend their market in otherwise restrictive countries.

II. CONSUMER AND PRODUCER

May 1970 saw the first confrontation between representatives of the various European consumer organisations and Europe's airline chiefs.[2] Both sides predictably claimed to be spokesman for the consumer, both sides claimed unique knowledge of his interests. It became clear that each party was catering for different consumers.

Conflicting views of consumer demand

The consumer organisations wanted lower fares and argued that they would extend the market and bring an era of mass air travel nearer in Europe. The airlines considered the consumer wanted a 'public service': planes flown at regular and frequent pre-determined times regardless of pay loads. In short, the airlines pointed out that costs could be reduced only at some sacrifice in service and convenience. It is evident that half-empty planes are not necessarily a sign of inefficiency or mismanagement, they are rather part of the airlines' service to the public. If the consumer wants to book late on a flight he knows will take off at the advertised time, and stretch out

[1] Cmnd. 4527, 1970.
[2] 'Can we have Mass Air Travel in Europe?', Symposium at the Gottlieb Duttweiler Institute, Zurich, 21 and 22 May, 1970.

across two seats, and receive prompt service from his air hostess, he must be prepared in effect to pay for two seats. But does he want this? The consumer organisations thought not. They favoured the lowest possible fare consistent with maximum safety.

The truth is that neither of these two consumers exist. All consumers have only one characteristic in common—*the desire for choice*. Some of us some of the time desire relatively low-cost 'inconvenient' flights, and at other times relatively high-cost 'convenient' flights. The present system offers consumers virtually no significant choice, and forces them to accept high prices and almost complete uniformity of product.

Effects of producers' cartel

Scheduled international civil aviation is organised through a producers' cartel (IATA).[1] Periodically, representatives of the world's 100 major airlines meet behind locked doors and decide all fare structures and the general quality of service and comfort in the plane cabin (width of seat, pitch,[2] free gifts, food, leg room, etc.). The method adopted is one of complete unanimity between member airlines: all must agree each decision. Given identical fares and services, what remains of competition?

(a) Product differentiation

The principal possibilities for product differentiation are type of aircraft and load factor. All airlines are anxious to fly the most advanced planes. As soon as one airline introduces a new type of plane, or there is a danger that it might, others feel competitively compelled to follow. Old and not so old planes are written off before they are fully depreciated and 'technological progress' is made in the absence of any indication of cost-related consumer demand for it.

Airlines fight for market shares by high selling-cost outlays (as high as Air India's 30 per cent of operating revenue) which search for points of product differentiation (Table II). Pan Am has emphasised that it was first with the 747, Iran Air tells the would-be traveller he will have plenty of room, not be 'sand-

---

[1] A producers' association which has the primary purpose of fixing prices at a level acceptable to all members.
[2] The 'pitch' is the distance between the edge of a seat and the edge of the one in front with both seats in the upright position. This must be no more than 34in. economy class and 42in. first class.

wiched between two strangers' with 'air hostesses taking twenty minutes to deliver a second coffee'. The *Economist* often carries up to 14 full pages of advertising matter for international airlines.

TABLE II

TICKETING, SALES AND PROMOTION AS A
PROPORTION OF TOTAL REVENUE, 1967

Air India	29
Lufthansa	25
SAS	22
Alitalia	22
KLM	22
Swissair	21
BOAC	21
TWA	19
Irish	18
Pan Am	17
Pakistan	11

Source: ICAO, *Digest of Statistics—Financial Data*, 1967.

The result has been high-cost flying with little choice. A cartel is an economic organisation *designed* to protect excess capacity. Fares are agreed which will keep the current firms and their planes 'in the air'. Indeed, by restricting quality variations as well as prices, IATA encourages *additional* excess capacity. New planes and empty seats, by providing additional comfort, are themselves competitive weapons which differentiate the product.

(b) *Excess capacity*
Excess capacity adds to costs and thus to prices. Increases in prices reduce the potential market. The result of a system in which prices must cover the least efficient flier is that despite an 11-fold increase in passengers carried since 1948 and a 15-fold increase in passenger kilometres the airlines are in dire financial trouble. Whilst over the past three years operating revenue increased at 14 per cent, operating costs have been increasing at 17 per cent. Profits of the leading 10 carriers in the US have fallen from over $400 million to an estimated $50 million loss in under three years. The world average passenger-load factor has fallen from 61 per cent in 1957 to just over 50 per cent in 1969.

The producers' cartel results in uniform prices and quality. Both of these would equally result from a monopoly but with

[16]

the difference that a monopoly airline would offer at least an *opportunity* for rationalisation, economies of scale and the elimination of excess capacity. In short, a monopoly would hold the promise of lower costs. *A cartel is a device for maintaining costs.*

Economic model of an airline cartel

In practice this producers' cartel is a good deal more inefficient than most because there is complete freedom of entry to it. New airlines are positively encouraged to join. Each new entry adds to capacity and necessitates higher prices to cover costs and to account for the resulting fall in load factors. As G. L. Bach has put it in another context:

> 'such a cartel arrangement with free entry, it might be argued, is not a halfway point between competition and monopoly, but rather an arrangement that combines the worst characteristics of each and the benefits of neither'.[1]

Assuming a simple model with only 10 airlines, what would be the long-run implications of their establishing a cartel to agree on prices and to share the market? Providing that they could prevent further airlines from entering they would act as a monopolist and set fares so as to maximise their collective profits. Assume that the fare in a competitive market would be £400 (i.e., the lowest point on each airline's total unit cost curve). At a fare of £400 there would be 30,000 travellers. If the numbers travelling were restricted to 20,000, however, the airlines could charge £500 and make £75 on each ticket sold (Diagram 1). At £500 the fare is higher than the competitive one, output is lower and production less efficient (i.e., at a higher cost per unit).

Suppose, however, that new airlines can freely join the cartel. Total sales will be divided up amongst more and more companies until (or perhaps even beyond) the point where costs are equal to £500. With 15 airlines in the market, each will sell only 1,333 tickets and costs will equal revenue. Consumers are just as badly off as with only 10 airlines since fares remain at £500 and output is still restricted to 20,000 trips. Airlines are no better off than under a competitive system but consumers suffer all the consequences of monopoly and over-investment. Indeed, under a single-firm monopoly economies

G. L. Bach, *Economics*, Prentice-Hall, 6th edition, 1968, p. 364.

of scale might have lowered the entire cost curve so that profits would have resulted at a fare of £400.

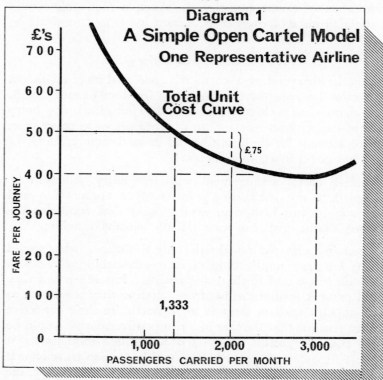

Diagram 1
A Simple Open Cartel Model
One Representative Airline

Total Unit Cost Curve

Airlines are collectively price makers and they will in practice 'make' their prices such that capacity additions, errors, and inefficiency are covered by price adjustments. *They have no incentive to minimise costs.*

The responsibility for this unhappy situation lies with governments. By controlling the sovereignty of their airspace they have collectively the power to create whatever world market structure they like. In practice governments have negotiated a complex set of bilateral agreements governing frequency and routes between their countries. They usually retain the right to veto air fares, but fare-fixing has in practice been delegated to national airlines. States merely rubber-stamp IATA agreements. In the past the American Civil Aeronautics Board (CAB) has been a noble exception to this passive policy.

Once the governments of the world had abandoned freedom

[18]

of the air and opted for negotiated bilateral agreements, the IATA system was inevitable. IATA is simply the secretariat of its 100 or so members. It has no policy save that unanimously agreed by its members.

Even without government intervention, price stability and price leadership would probably be inevitable. By its nature international aviation is highly oligopolostic.[1] Concentration ratios are very high and entry barriers formidable. Further there has been a complete dearth of useable alternatives—the general opinion has been that, although unsatisfactory, the present system is the only one 'politically viable'.

III. ELEMENTS OF COMPETITION

(i) *Within IATA*

It is argued that IATA is in some sense 'competitive' in that all airlines are interested in expanding both the total market and their share of it, and thus that there are strong pressures within IATA to get fares down. The potential is obvious; after all, less than one in ten Europeans fly. The argument runs that the inefficient airlines must compromise at the IATA conference table or risk a rates-war outside the cartel. In the main, however, the potentially efficient have preferred to inflate costs by purchasing bigger and faster (and better?) planes to attract trade away from the small rather than struggle for decreases in fares. In any event, to break away is not easy because other members have their governments behind them, and they could withdraw landing rights from the offending airline.

The irrationality of pretending that IATA is in any sense competitive emerges nicely from a consideration of the speech by Mr Keith Granville (now chairman of BOAC) to the International Aviation Club in the USA in 1969. The basic conditions of the Bermuda agreement (the inter-governmental agreement governing conditions of flight on the North Atlantic), he said, were that the 'carriers of one country should not unduly affect the services of airlines of the other country on the agreed

---

[1] *Oligopoly:* A market situation where there are only a few firms of comparable importance in the production of a commodity, so that each must anticipate the reactions of the others to any change in an economic variable that it makes.

routes'. This is an accurate assessment, but one scarcely supporting the 'competitive' hypothesis.

Mr Granville's concern was that, with fixed prices and quality of provision, Pan Am and TWA were attempting to 'compete' traffic away from BOAC by 'swamping the North Atlantic route with capacity'. Clearly with so little to choose between airlines, the more flights any one airline has, the larger the share of any given market it stands to get. Frequency of flights, however, is in theory a matter of negotiation between governments: hence Mr Granville's protest. To retaliate, he claimed, would in any event reduce both parties' pay-loads to 30 per cent. If it continued the whole agreement would have to be reconsidered:

'We cannot contemplate our hard-won prosperity being set at risk by your airlines on routes where, in future, an increasing proportion of our total capacity will be deployed. Nor can we put at risk our ability to recoup the huge dollar investments we have made in the 747s'.

So much for competition within IATA—it is just not part of the current institutional framework.[1]

Occasionally competition breaks out which if not outside the letter of IATA rules is certainly outside their spirit. One air line has offered subsidized car rentals for travellers from outside Europe, whilst another has offered sight-seeing tours. Further stories of 'over-generous' commission to travel agents from some European lines abound in the trade.

(ii) *Outside IATA*

In the formal sense at least not all international fares come under the IATA umbrella. Planes may be chartered to third parties or may carry passengers who have purchased a 'package tour'. These forms of flying are in practice substitutes for

[1] Mr Keith Granville (then Managing Director, BOAC) quoted in the *Financial Times*, 22 November, 1969. The facts that caused Mr Granville's concern were that the US lines were flying 178 flights a week to the UK which represented 45 per cent of all their traffic on their trans-Atlantic services. In contrast the US–UK segment of the traffic was only 28 per cent of the total market. 52 per cent of their UK flights went on to Europe having 'topped-up' with local UK—Europe passengers. We have no quarrel with Mr Granville's position or facts; we quote him merely to illustrate how far from the scene in practice is the concept of 'competing'. In the event route swamping has cost Pan Am a deterioration in load factor and, as a consequence, profitability.

schedule airline flying, although how close is debatable. Increasingly, however, 'affinity' group charters and tours are providing services which are relatively regular and systematic and which sell to almost anyone prepared to put himself to a minimum of inconvenience to find out about them.

Competition from both these sources has, so far, been in no sense 'free'. Charter flights are, in theory at least, restricted to groups formed for non-travel purposes ('affinity groups') and open only to members of at least six months standing. On the other hand, prices of package tours have been related, in this country, by the Board of Trade to IATA fares. Until recently the cost of the holiday could not be less than the normal return-trip IATA fare. For winter holidays of short duration this protection has been relaxed on some European routes, despite opposition from the scheduled airlines. As a result Sky Tours have been able to offer a four-day holiday in Majorca for £18. This budgets £9.50 return a head for the flight on a Britannia Airways 737 jet. The total cost of the holiday including all meals, accommodation and the flight comes to over £12 less than the scheduled single fare. This includes a profit element for both the airline and the travel group (which are under the same management). In practice the attempt to enforce a minimum package-tour price has been frustrated by some holiday companies which offer vouchers entitling the holders to free excursions, drinks and car hire. Although this practice is now officially banned it is difficult to see what can prevent tour operators from arranging for foreign hoteliers to issue them to visitors on arrival.

'Affinity group' chartering

'Affinity group' chartering is open to any society which has been in existence for two years and has less than 20,000 members.[1] Over the last 10 years this type of flying has expanded at a very high rate. For example, 55 per cent of the North Atlantic passenger air traffic to and from Canada now comprises affinity group charters. Although IATA rules forbid any advertising of these trips beyond the confines of the clubs, in practice they are widely canvassed. The Jet Charter Advice Bureau (which has advertised in *Punch*), the Lower Fare

[1] The IATA rule is less than 50,000 members but the British Government imposes a more restrictive version of the rule.

League and the Charter Flight Information Centre all exist to centralise information about affinity group charter flights.

It has become big business. Although few of the general public have heard of it, World Airways, one of the largest charter companies, is bigger than Qantas or Swissair. The second largest, Overseas National, carries ¼-million people across the North Atlantic alone. Other large charter companies include Caledonian, Trans-International and Capitol. One of Overseas National's recent trade advertisements runs:

'If you can get 250 nudists together, Overseas National Airways will fly them from London to New York at a basically bare £52 each—so you don't know any nudists? Then get 250 bishops or boy scouts together'.

World Airways recently found a legitimate loophole in the IATA regulations by discovering that any business company could hire a plane and sell tickets to its employees without restrictions. At least one firm is now taking advantage of this facility.

Any copy of *The Times* offers charter trips to most places in the world, not always adding 'for members'. Tour companies' advertisements point out that businessmen can use their package travel, hotel and meal service to, say, the Far East, and still save substantial sums on the scheduled fare, for example, £160 on a trip to Japan. The normal economy class fare from London to Tokyo is £564 70p, whereas group contract fares go as low as £230 in winter.

The Board of Trade adds the spice of excitement to flying with such charters by occasionally warning airlines that the club it is chartering has 'bent' the rules. Airlines have then to withdraw their services or risk losing what is in effect their 'licence to land'.

By and large, however, it is possible to fly with a charter to most main centres of the world providing the passenger is prepared to commit himself to a date fairly far in advance, although a recent survey by *Which?* suggested that it was 'easy' to change the date up to six weeks before the flight.[1] The clubs are mainly travel clubs with a different window dressing. *Which?* found 50 per cent of their 360 sample had never

[1] *Which?*, January 1971.

attended the club before flying. The IATA rule is that members must have attended at least six meetings of the club, although they may of course *book* a flight on joining the society.

It is also equally clear that several clubs are being used as a means of making quick money out of so-called non-profit-making societies. It remains basically absurd to the man in the street that a £2 membership of a bird-watching society should yield him a £60–£70 saving in crossing the Atlantic. Indeed the future promises further fare cuts by charter companies. A Boeing 747 with 395 members on board could cross both ways for £34 a head.

Variations in fares

Table III illustrates the wide discrepancies in fares for nine key routes. Such large discrepancies need explanation. Charter fares out of London per mile range from 2.0 old pence (e.g., New York, Toronto, Los Angeles) to 3.4 old pence (e.g., Sydney). This compares with normal scheduled rates of 5.0 to 12.0 old pence per mile (e.g., Milan) and with the Skyways holiday package fare to Majorca of 1.4 old pence. Hitherto the scheduled lines have tried to have their cake and eat it. They argue the reason for these low rates is that the charter product is very different. The flights only take place full,[1] at predetermined outgoing and incoming times and dates, and that there are no free last-minute cancellation rights nor rights to vary routes and stop-overs. On the other hand, it is argued by airlines that the rationale for tying holiday rates to IATA fares and for maintaining the affinity rules is that the product offered is similar, and that the scheduled airlines would not be able to compete without them. Put another way, *if allowed the choice* passengers would opt for low cost (but more inconvenient) plane seats.

There is evidence that charter flights have a salutary deflating effect on scheduled airfares where they have a sizeable share of the market. The authors have found elsewhere[2] that there was a significant correlation coefficient of —0.8 between

---

[1] We have no evidence to support this oft repeated claim. Certainly the best weight load-factor that the scheduled airlines can achieve on *their* own charter services is 73 per cent (cf. 52 per cent for all scheduled services). This is a long way short of the assertions made in reference to their competitors. In 1969 UK inclusive tour operators had load-factors ranging from 73 to 92 per cent.

[2] M. H. Cooper and A. K. Maynard, '*The Effect of Regulated Competition on 'Scheduled Air Fares*' (forthcoming).

TABLE III
SCHEDULED/NON SCHEDULED FARE CONTRASTS

Destination	Return Scheduled Fare £	Return Average Charter Fare £	Saving %
Sydney*	580	320	45
Toronto	183	65	64
Nairobi	296	100	66
Hong Kong	485	160	67
Singapore	424	150	65
Bombay	319	145	54
Delhi	319	120	64
New York	175	60	66
Los Angeles	293	95	67

Source: Various.
* Fare fixed by Australian Government at 55 per cent of scheduled fare. Charter must be from BOAC or Qantas.

both normal scheduled fares and the percentage of the market held by charter flight companies, and between the latter and special 'promotional' fares. Despite similar load factors the scheduled fare per kilometre to Copenhagen is 7.80 old pence, to Ibiza 5.40 old pence. Charter airlines have only 11 per cent of the Copenhagen traffic but 82 per cent of that to Ibiza.

Airline revenue is further diluted on these 'holiday' routes because ITX fares[1] (fares charged to the holiday tour companies and not available to the public direct) in effect have to reflect charter rates, as do special excursion and 'promotional' fares. These package-tour rates have caused considerable resentment amongst the business community as full-fare passengers find themselves sitting next to bargain ITX ticket-holders. Indeed there have been recent complaints of over-booking because tour parties refuse to be divided between flights. Regular ticket-holders frequently find airlines giving preference to groups and connecting passengers.

(iii) Price discrimination

Fares per kilometre vary widely. Dr Arne Rosenberg in his study of European air services has constructed an index showing a variation from 15 per cent below to 36 per cent above the

---

[1] These ITX fares tend to be automatically sanctioned by the Board of Trade as the tour operator could turn to a foreign airline.

average.[1] All fares on average were 55 per cent higher than those within the USA, a contrast which to some extent is explained by the higher costs implicit in short-haul flying. In such cases, fuel, depreciation and ground costs are bound to be higher (Table IV).

TABLE IV

THE ROSENBERG INDEX

Fares per kilometre (Average 100)

Short distance over Alps	136
Turkey—W. Europe	130–135
Scandinavia—Continent	125–130
Greece—W. Europe	110–115
Scandinavia—UK	110–115
London—Continent	105–110
Within Scandinavia	105–110
UK (except London)—Continent	90–95
UK—Spain and Portugal	90–95
Within Continent (except Alps)	90–95
UK—Ireland	85–90
Holland—Rest of Continent	85–90
North Africa—W. Europe	85–90
USA internal	50
Australia internal	50

Source: A. Rosenberg, *Air Travel Within Europe*,
National Swedish Consumer Council, 1970.

Further, many prices can be offered for a given journey to a usually bewildered consumer. There are, for example, over 30 possible fares for a flight from San Francisco to London. The complexities of ticket prices are such that an expert is needed to find his way through the small print. Mostly prices have no obvious or consistent relationship to costs or mileage. Many have been decided *ad hoc* outside the IATA Conference by the interested airlines in cohort (usually two, infrequently, as on the North Atlantic, by as many as 20). The logic of many fares is obscured by history. It is, for example, dearer per kilometre to fly over water, because the original intention was to price competitively with first-class rail. Again the old non-pressurised cabins necessitated flying around the Alps and today's fares still reflect the no-longer-flown extra mileage.

[1] A. Rosenberg, *Air Travel Within Europe*, National Swedish Consumer Council, 1970.

Fares and elasticity of demand

The irony of this situation is that despite the enormous variation of fares at varying times of day, year and for varying lengths of stay, and between different routes of the same mileage, little competitive element has been introduced. All fare variations are common, at least in principle, to all airlines serving the two points in question. Nor is there any evidence that the fare variations reflect demand elasticities, in any necessarily consistent manner.[1] Fares vary often in the face of, and despite, demand conditions rather than because of them. They often reflect supplier convenience rather than consumer sovereignty.

Studies in the early 1960s by Dr S. Wheatcroft among others suggest large variations in the elasticity of demand between groups of traveller, for example, those visiting friends and relations 2.20; holiday makers 2.00; and business men 0.70.[2] Price discrimination aimed at exploiting these differences is, of course, not easy because business men at present will, for example, take advantage of ITX fares wherever possible (i.e., fly as holiday makers to do business in e.g., the Far East). With so small a portion of the potential business market touched, it is difficult to think that the inelasticity of demand from this section of the market is anything more than a reflection of the segment of the demand curve currently being tapped.

Dr Wheatcroft also suggested that the elasticity of demand was larger in the summer (1.8) than in the winter (1.6), but of course any attempt to reflect this difference in pricing would increase the peaking problem. More recently Dr M. R. Straszheim has put the average elasticity at 1.5 for the North Atlantic and up to 2.0 for Europe.[3]

The translation of common tariff prices into different currencies at the going exchange rates is another aspect of the same problem. Exchange rates do not reflect purchasing-power parity. One pound sterling will not necessarily buy in the US the same amount of goods and services as would $2.40, despite the exchange rate of £1 = $2.40. The exchange rate of a given currency tends to reflect the external demand for it rather than its internal value in real terms. The result is that the expansion of air travel is unintentionally hindered in some countries. The

[1] 'Elasticity' is a measure that tells how much the quantity bought will change in response to a (small) change in price. Thus, demand elasticity is a measure of the responsiveness of quantity bought to (small) changes in price.
[2] Cited by R. Colgate, Zurich Symposium, *op. cit.*
[3] M. R. Straszheim, *op. cit.*

[26]

trans-Atlantic fare to America reflects only some 2.5 per cent of American average incomes but nearly 5 per cent to the British would-be traveller. Clearly bringing the proportional relationships into line by freely flexible exchange rates would considerably increase the British market.

Another source of discrimination which causes much resentment in Europe is the so-called '20 per cent' rule which allows route variations up to 20 per cent of the direct mileage at no further charge. The result is that US visitors to Europe in effect fly free this side of the Atlantic, and thus cause considerable revenue dilution and necessitate higher scheduled fares in Europe to cover costs.

IV. COSTS, REVENUE AND FARES

Over the period 1951–68 costs per kilometre-ton performed dropped by 25 per cent, whilst costs per kilometre-ton available but partly utilised dropped by 36 per cent. The revenue per kilometre-ton received by airlines for passenger conveyance, however, fell only marginally from 43.6 cents to 40.2 cents, despite considerable revenue dilution due to the decline in first-class passengers from 21 per cent of the total traffic in 1958 to only 7 per cent in 1968, and the introduction of special excursion and other promotional fares in 1963. Falling load-factors and a large drop in mail revenue, however, effectively prevented profits from improving significantly. Revenue per kilometre-ton from mail was 66.7 cents in 1951 but only 28.3 by 1968 (Table V). The net margin in 1951 of 0.5 cents per kilometre-ton improved over the period to 2.9 cents.

TABLE V
WORLD SCHEDULED AIRLINES' COSTS AND
REVENUES, 1951 AND 1968
(US cents)

	1951	1968
Costs per kilometre-ton performed	40.4	30.5
Costs per kilometre-ton available	25.2	16.0
Revenue per kilometre-ton performed	40.9	33.4
Passengers only	43.6	40.2
Non-scheduled flights	32.6	16.4
Mail	66.7	28.3
Revenue per kilometre-ton available	25.6	17.5

Source: ICAO, *Digest of Statistics, Financial Data* 1967, p. 26.

By the end of the period nearly half of the ICAO fleets were jets, and the airlines had fully absorbed their impact, employing them for 86 per cent of the total hours flown. Since 1968 all the evidence is that a combination of inflation and the introduction of the 747 'jumbo' jet has narrowed the margin once more to a fraction of a cent.

The US airlines are reported to be speculating on the probable size of their losses for 1971. Both BEA and BOAC report a drastic reduction in profitability for the first halves of their current financial years. Costs in 1969 grew 2 per cent faster than revenue. Some airlines are reacting by cutting back the frequency of their services to reduce costs.

Table VI examines the cost and revenue performance of 14 airlines. One of the most striking observations to be made is the enormous variation in cents per kilometre-ton performed. The range in 1967 was from 20.8 cents to 63.1 cents. Still more remarkable is that the level of costs is apparently always covered by revenue. Indeed, of the leading 10 airlines only Air France dropped below break-even point between 1963 and 1968. This is, of course, exactly what one would predict as the outcome of IATA pricing policy.

Profitability not related to efficiency

The third column in Table VI shows profitability. These figures include varying degrees of subsidisation (both explicit and implicit) from their respective governments and are not strictly comparable with the figures in columns 1 and 2. Nevertheless, they clearly show that amongst the rewards of efficiency, enhanced profitability is strangely missing. Pan Am has the lowest costs but also the lowest revenue: BOAC, Irish International and TWA were similarly affected. Pan Am's seemingly low-cost record appears all the more remarkable after allowance for their relatively high average wages. The reason appears to lie in enhanced labour efficiency. Each Pan Am staff member handles 169 more passengers, implying 65 per cent more miles flown, than his BOAC counter-part, and this despite the average BOAC flight being 60 per cent longer.

Profit and loss seem to have little to do with efficiency but much with flying 'prestigious' and remunerative routes.

Although BUA has managed to make profits for the last five years out of the Latin American routes BOAC gave up as

TABLE VI

OPERATING COST AND REVENUE ACCOUNTS: SELECTED AIRLINES, 1960 AND 1967

Cents per kilometre-ton performed

	Costs		Revenue		Profits and Subsidies	
	1960	*1967*	*1960*	*1967*	*1960*	*1967*
Pan Am	36.9	20.8	39.1	23.5	1.3	2.5
TWA	37.7	28.6	39.4	30.4	1.6	2.0
BOAC	43.4	30.4	45.7	35.0	—1.2	2.7
Air France	53.4	39.6+	52.6	41.7+	0.1	0.9
Lufthansa	54.7	36.2	48.5	36.9	0.0	0.7
Air India	44.4*	32.3	46.0	35.8	1.0	2.3
Lebanon—Middle East	67.7	47.3	70.8	49.2	0.5	0.9
JAL	40.6*	35.0	42.7*	36.9	0.2	0.6
Philippines	34.5	36.9	36.6	40.6	1.6	3.5
Peru	n.a.	33.2	n.a.	33.5	—0.2	0.5
Luxair	n.a.	63.1	88.4°	43.7	n.a.	—4.7
Icelandic	32.0*	47.0	34.8	46.5	—1.0	—2.7
Irish International	45.3	25.7	43.5	28.7	—1.8	2.5
Aer Lingus	46.4	55.4	49.2	54.7	2.0	—2.4

+ 1965
* 1961
• 1963
Source: ICAO, Various publications on financial data.

white elephants, Pan Am continues to incur losses serving Latin America but makes a profit of 3.8 cents on the Pacific. These Pacific fares are high enough not only to yield Pan Am a margin but also to cover JAL's relatively higher costs.

In addition to the large variation in costs *between* airlines, they are generally high relative to Caledonian's charter costs of around 16 cents per kilometre-ton on short-haul European flights. Further, BUA's cost conditions are such that it can make profits on the London–Belfast route with a load factor of only 46 per cent, whilst BEA loses money with a load factor of 71 per cent. If, however, as shown in Table VII, the scheduled airlines' costs per kilometre-ton *available* (flown, including empty seats) is contrasted with their revenue per kilometre-ton *performed* (occupied seats), the scope for fare reductions from filling more seats or cutting back empty capacity is very striking. Pan Am are managing to service the world's airports at a cost per kilometre-ton of only 11.9 cents.

Assuming even an 80 per cent load-factor, and converting

[29]

kilometre-tons into passenger-kilometres at 10 passengers to a ton, fare levels of 3 cents a kilometre appear feasible, that is, some one-third or less of current normal scheduled fares.

TABLE VII

COSTS PER KILOMETRE-TON AVAILABLE AND
REVENUE PER KILOMETRE-TON PERFORMED:
SELECTED AIRLINES, 1960 AND 1967

	Costs cents per kilometre-ton available		Revenue cents per kilometre-ton performed	
	1960	*1967*	*1960*	*1967*
Pan Am	21.9	11.9	39.1	23.5
TWA	20.3	13.0	39.4	30.4
BOAC	25.7	16.1	45.7	35.0
Air France	32.7	23.3+	52.6	41.7+
Lufthansa	30.7	19.9	48.5	36.9
Air India	20.2*	15.9	46.0	35.8
Lebanese—Middle East	26.9	26.2	70.8	49.2
JAL	24.7*	20.6	42.7	36.9
Philippines	23.6	18.2	36.6	40.6
Peru	n.a.	18.6	n.a.	33.5
Luxair	39.5°	32.0	88.4°	43.7
Icelandic	20.3*	25.3	34.8	46.5
Irish International	27.4	16.7	43.5	28.7
Aer Lingus	30.0	32.9	49.2	54.7

+ 1965
° 1963
* 1961
Source: ICAO, Various publications on financial data.

Have fares gone down?

Giving the 1970 Brancker Memorial Lecture, Mr Knut Hammarskjold, the Secretary General of IATA, stated:

'By and large I believe that the IATA fare structure has been successful in developing air passenger travel and in opening up the air travel market to larger numbers of people at lower and lower fares. Overseas travel is no longer reserved for the wealthy visitor but has become within easy reach of the "medium income bracket" tourist'.[1]

[1] Knut Hammarskjold, '70s Challenging Years for the World Air Transport System'. *Institute of Transport Journal*, May, 1970.

Two observations suggest themselves. First, less than 10 per cent of Europeans fly, and the development of the medium-income bracket tourist trade has been at the initiative of tour operators and charter groups rather than due to IATA tariffs. Second, is it even true that flying is at 'lower and lower fares'? 1971 fares have been announced as 8 per cent higher than 1970.

IATA's evidence for its claim was that 'the lowest available normal New York to London return fare has been reduced from 1951's $711 to $420 in 1969'. Although literally true this statement is extremely misleading. The selection of one route, and that one on which over 20 airlines 'compete' is hardly representative. Even more misleading is to fail to mention that in 1950 and 1951 there existed only one class of flight.

The choice of 1951 as a base for comparison with 1969 is again unfortunate. Normal fares (first class only) peaked in that year at $711. In 1946 they were $586 or £145 at the then rate of exchange. IATA also failed to point out that there was also a fare of $412 available in that same year—$8 under the figure mentioned for 1969. Further the reduction of the seat pitch from 39 in. to 34 in. and of meals to buffet snacks in 1958 are strangely missing from references to 'improved standards of service'. Comparing like with like, the return first-class fare in 1970 was £312 and the one-class fare in 1950, £225. Further, the return off-season fare in 1950 was £167 whilst the return off-season economy fare following British devaluation is now £174. Admittedly in real terms the cost of crossing the Atlantic has fallen but whether sufficiently to bring travel within the grasp of the medium-income bracket is a moot point. In contrast the return fare by charter is at most £60 and could be as low as £35.

Comparison of fares over time is complicated and the result uncertain. There are some 60,000 possible fares, and often several routes linking two centres. Further, the classes of travel have undergone changes and with them standards of comfort and amenities. Table VIII compares normal fares over 20 years for five important international services. In each case the mileage taken is that of the shortest route. The single first-class fare is today dearer in money terms in all but one case. Certainly there is no evidence of wholesale reductions in fare levels.

[31]

TABLE VIII

SELECTED NORMAL FARES, 1950 and 1970

	Mileage		Old pence per mile 1950	Old pence per mile 1970
London—Sydney	11,235			
First		Single	5.5	9.7
Economy		Single	N.A.	6.1
First		Return	5.0	9.7
Economy		Return	N.A.	6.1
London—New York	3,456			
First		Single	8.6	10.8
Economy High Season		Single	8.6	7.3
		Return	7.8	7.3
Low Season		Return	5.7	6.0
London—Tokyo	9,115			
First		Single	5.7	12.3
Economy		Single	N.A.	7.4
First		Return	4.7	12.3
Economy		Return	N.A.	7.4
Rome—New York	4,280			
First		Single	10.2	9.3
Economy High Season		Single	10.2	6.6
		Return	7.8	6.6
Low Season		Return	6.1	5.7
Hong Kong—Honolulu	5,637			
First		Single	8.9	11.4
Economy		Single	N.A.	6.9
First		Return	8.4	10.9
Economy		Return	N.A.	6.7

Source: *ABC World Airways Guides*.
'N.A.': Not available as there was no economy class in 1950 on these routes.

The more striking observation from Table VIII is, as we have already observed for Europe in Table IV, the enormous variation in fares per mile between different routes. The range, although less than in 1950, is nevertheless from 6.1 old pence per mile economy to 7.4 old pence per mile economy. Some European economy-class fares exceed one shilling per mile: for example, Algiers to Palma, London to Milan, and Athens to Munich. Again internal African flights can be found at fares of over 1s 4d a mile: for example, Doule to Lagos or Dar Es Salaam to Entebbe. At the other end of the spectrum, the fare from

London to Honolulu is only 5.6 old pence per mile. It could be argued, of course, that these fare differentials reflect (a) exogeneous cost variations, (b) elasticities of demand, or (c) both. Equally they could reflect (a) inefficient high-cost flying on the Pacific runs, (b) duopoly profits, (c) the outcome of stalemate bargaining at the IATA Tariff Conferences, and (d) all three. On the circumstantial evidence available we can see no reason to prefer the first set of explanations.

Any given fare settled at the IATA Conference table could represent profits to one airline, losses to another in capacity trouble, and still be considerably in excess of the charter fare even after the addition of a profit mark-up.

Excursions and 'promotional' fares

So far we have concerned ourselves with three forms of air travel:

(1) scheduled air flights at normal first and economy fares (high or low season);

(2) ITX package tour fares on scheduled flights;

(3) charter group fares (which may or may not be on planes owned by scheduled airlines).

A sizeable proportion of the scheduled airlines' passenger traffic, however, travels at rates below the normal category (1) fare and does not fit into either categories (2) or (3). On the North Atlantic, for example, only 60 per cent of the scheduled traffic pays normal scheduled fares, 29 per cent the so-called excursion fares and 11 per cent other 'promotional' fares. The first group is thought by airlines to correspond roughly to business travel where a third party is paying the bill and where the demand is relatively inelastic. The second and third groups consist of holiday-makers travelling on their own and the timorous making a first trip by air, lured by 'special offers' to visit friends and places. In practice, however, these fares are badly publicised, ill-understood and a cause of considerable irritation to seasoned travellers. These fares can vary with the time of day or night, a minimum or maximum length of stay, and are available only on certain stated routes.

They were introduced on the North Atlantic routes in 1963 in direct response to a then current load-factor of only 49 per cent, and have remained ever since undergoing many modifica-

[33]

tions but with a gradual decline in level. Many airlines attribute the growth of traffic from 2.4 million to 5 million between 1963 and 1967 to these low 'bargain' fares. Of course this attempt to counter charter competition added to the fall in revenue resulting from the decline of first-class travel.

Against a background of relatively stable and often increasing normal fares, excursion fares have fallen but remained well above the charter rates. In 1968 the scheduled air traffic's growth rate dropped away and there was a general move (resisted only by the small national prestige airlines) to reduce excursion fares still more. In September 1969 Alitalia unexpectedly announced that it would cut its Rome–New York excursion fare by £41 to £123 return. There immediately followed 175 revised fare proposals for IATA to contend with. BOAC, Pan Am, TWA and Aer Lingus all matched Alitalia's fare level almost immediately. The most dramatic departure, however, came from Air Canada who proposed to abandon the 'affinity group' IATA rules and fly any 50 people who 'turned up in a group at the airport' for £102-35 Montreal to London return each. In the event opposition to Air Canada's proposals from some European members of IATA ensured it was still-born.

Following much publicity and several IATA meetings a compromise agreement was reached. A return excursion fare for stays abroad of between three weeks and 49 days was agreed and the old excursion period of 14 to 21 days was extended to 28 days. IATA surprisingly regarded this as a tremendous break for tourists hunting air-fare 'bargains'. The press generally hailed it as a fare cut resulting from competition. *In the event scheduled first-class and economy fares had not been changed at all.* The final agreement was for excursion fares of £104 in winter, £110 in spring and £123 in summer,[1] a far cry from charter rates ranging from £38 in winter to £60 in summer.

Nevertheless the differentials between these excursion rates and the £174 economy fare have been wide enough to make some business men buy an excursion ticket in London and another one in New York, using them alternatively in order to beat the minimum stay requirement.

[1] Peaking in common with most forms of transport is a most serious problem. On the North Atlantic, east-bound traffic for example is some four-fold higher in July than in February.

Again, despite these excursion offers, charter business has continued to flourish, whilst the scheduled airlines' stake in chartering has remained small. In the world market some 6 per cent of the scheduled airlines' flights are currently on charter business. On the North Atlantic $7\frac{1}{2}$ per cent of their flights were charters in 1959 but only 6 per cent in 1969. The number of passengers carried, however, went up proportionately from 11 to $11\frac{1}{2}$ per cent and amounted to 780,000 passengers in 1969. The very large increase in 1969 was in the event exceeded by the non-scheduled charter traffic, which increased by 87 per cent (Table IX).

TABLE IX

GROWTH OF CHARTER PASSENGERS CARRIED ON N. ATLANTIC BY SCHEDULED AIRLINES (IATA MEMBERS)
(per cent)

1964	1965	1966	1967	1968	1969
+ 16.4	− 0.3	+ 4.7	+ 2.8	− 4.2	+ 57.5

Source: IATA, *World Air Transport Statistics No.* 14, 1969 (1970).

Between 1964 and 1968 the number of passengers flown on scheduled charter fluctuated, actually decreasing in 1965 and 1968. Indeed this is symptomatic of the scheduled airlines' attitude to chartering: an attempt to beat them rather than join them. Fares have repeatedly been brought down as a *reaction* to charter activity—rarely if ever as a genuine initiative to create new markets. Indeed many of the scheduled airlines' initiatives have been followed by a price increase. The first pressurised cabin (the Constellation) and the 707's introduction both resulted in surcharges. Now TWA are pressing for a surcharge for the 747 on US domestic routes which they seek to justify on the grounds of 'greater luxury'. One airline is already considering a 100 per cent surcharge on Concorde although the plane would be profitable, given reasonable load factors, if passengers paid the current 'normal' fares. It is widely claimed that operating costs will be 100 per cent higher than for the 747 but with high load-factors the 747 could be viable at £34 return per seat on the North Atlantic. Doubling this figure still leaves a generous margin over the normal scheduled air fare.

[35]

The fares equation

No amount of special offers can disguise the fact that in the face of falling costs (25 per cent in 17 years) normal fares went up in 1963, and 1969, and again in 1971. IATA's claim that fares had become 'lower and lower' was made in terms of the 'lowest available *normal* New York–London return fare'. We must now ask whether the special offer excursions of the post-1969 period are lower in money terms than those of the immediate post-war era. The excursion fares in Table X

TABLE X

FARES ON NORTH ATLANTIC, NEW YORK–LONDON ROUTE, 1971

	$	£
Normal		
First Class (one way)*	391	162.9
Economy (tourist)*		
basic (one way)	226	94.1
peak (one way)	275	114.5
Promotional		
Excursion (round-trip)*		
17–28 days		
basic	322	134.1
peak	382	159.1
29–45 days		
basic	272	113.3
peak	332	138.3
Affinity Groups		
(40 passengers or more eastbound, 30 westbound) (round trip)*		
basic	217	90.4
peak	277	115.4
winter (Nov–March)	197	82.0
Inclusive Tours		
(round trip)		
basic	237	98.7
peak	302	125.8

* 15 per cent surcharge at weekends.
Source: *ABC World Airways Guides.*

can be compared with a special winter round-trip fare in 1948 of £116 for a 30-day maximum stay (the limit was extended to 60 days in 1949–50). In 1950 an all-season return (up to 15 days' stay) was offered at the single fare plus 10 per cent or

£137. In 1964 a 14–21 day round-trip was offered at £119. The truth is fares have fluctuated a good deal, whilst two British devaluations have put fares up in sterling terms. The choice of base year and of the fare to be contrasted is critical. The evidence is that the IATA claim, if more prudently restricted to real terms, has some validity.

Table X shows the current range of fares offered on the New York to London run. These 22 possible fares are a simplification of the 1969 fare structure and represent an increase of 4 per cent in first-class fares, 8 per cent in economy fare and approximately 10 per cent in promotional fares. Before these increases (which were more widespread than simply North Atlantic) the IATA index of average world scheduled fares was said to be 8.7 per cent down over the past 10 years. It must therefore be standing about evens now, even including promotional fares.[1]

Promotional fares show the same wide variability between routes as observed for normal fares. The London to New York excursion fare is 4.3 old pence per mile, the fare from London to Nairobi 6.5 pence. An 'affinity group' of 50 persons can fly to Montreal for 2.8 pence per mile, a group of 80 to New York for 2.5 pence, but to Tokyo for 3.3 pence.

V. MARKET STRUCTURE

(i) Total market

Civil aviation is a highly concentrated industry. The top three airlines account for some 32 per cent of all traffic, the top five for 43 per cent. The Americans own 62 per cent of the world's airfleet compared with Britain's 6 per cent. By origin 96 per cent of the planes in the air are American. Again almost 60 per cent of all scheduled traffic is American as against Britain's 4.7 per cent stake.

The top airlines of the world are listed in Table XI. Ranking has changed very little over the 15 years from 1951 to 1965, although Pan Am and BOAC's dominance has dropped appreciably, giving ground to Lufthansa and Alitalia. The result has been a considerable reduction in concentration at the top.

[1] K. Hammarskjold, reported in *The Times*, 27 October, 1970.

[37]

TABLE XI
DISTRIBUTION OF THE INTERNATIONAL AIR MARKET, 1951, 1957 and 1965

	1951 % Market	Rank	*1957* % Market	Rank	*1965* % Market	Rank
Pan Am	25.32	1	20.00	1	16.17	1
BOAC	13.27	2	10.13	2	8.89	2
Air France	6.89	4	7.65	4	6.89	3
TWA	5.87	5	4.95	6	5 80	4
KLM	9 49	3	9 34	3	5.27	5
Lufthansa	n.a.	—	1.93	10	4.92	6
Alitalia	0.39	13	1.43	13	4.13	7
SAS	5.59	6	6.26	5	3.66	8
Qantas	2.74	7	3.14	8	3.51	9
Swissair	1.78	8	3.72	7	2.95	10
JAL	n.a.	—	1.17	14	2.71	11
Air Canada	1.49	9	1.55	12	2.42	12
Sabena	1.57	10	2.17	9	2.13	13
Air India	1.07	11	1.73	11	1.57	14
El Al	0.072	12	0.57	15	1.54	15

Source: IATA *Bulletins.*

Table **XII** shows the extremes in average load-factors among IATA members. They are yet another indication of the variations in cost conditions encountered. Passengers on routes served by four airlines (Ethiopian, Air Mali, Mohawk and Garuda) are being asked in effect to buy three seats a trip.

TABLE XII
LOAD-FACTOR EXTREMES—ALL CARRIERS, ALL INTERNATIONAL SERVICES, 1969

Low	%	Kilometres flown (million)	High	%	Kilometres flown (million)
Ethiopian	24.7	7.0	Cubana	79.3	2.9
Air Mali	29.0	1.5	Cruzeiro	71.6	2.0
Mohawk	30.3	0.9	(Brazil)		
Garuda	32.3	5.4	Air Algerie	65.2	6.8
Saudi Arabian	36.0	5.9	BEA	60.9	65.3
Viasa	38.1	13.5	Indian Airlines	60.8	1.6
Middle-East	38.2	17.1	Flugfelag	60.1	1.9
Braniff	38.8	21.2	(Iceland)		
Finnair	39.3	11.7	El Al	59.5	25.7

Source: IATA, *World Air Transport Statistics*, 1969.

[38]

What guarantee has the world consumer that it is not their cost conditions which are determining route prices? Admittedly the large airlines are concentrated over the range 45 to 60 per cent, but for an average on all routes this implies enormous cost variations.

(ii) *The North Atlantic*

By far the most important market in the world is the North Atlantic route which accounts for 30 per cent of all international passenger-miles flown. Table XIII examines the US–Europe segment of this important but untypical market in some detail. It is the sole market in which so many airlines 'compete'.

Given that all 19 airlines are charging the same fares and for the most part flying similar and often identical aircraft offering virtually identical amenities, what determines the potential consumer's choice?

The issue is a complex one but the most important criteria must be the frequency of service. To a large extent flights create their own share of demand—a passenger is more likely to turn to the line known to fly several flights a day than one with three a week. Other factors will include:

(1) habit;

(2) hour of take-off most convenient to the customer in question—obviously the importance of this factor diminishes with the length of the intended journey and in any case airlines tend to bunch at critical times;

(3) national pride—Irish International and El Al's load-factors can be attributed to their nationals flying with their own line whenever possible;

(4) extra amenities—this is really restricted by IATA to the showing of films in flight: Pan Am, TWA and National all show films subject to a $2.50 in-flight charge forced upon them by the other IATA members;

(5) recent safety record—although this probably applies as much to the type of plane as to the airline;

(6) load-factor—the likelihood of getting two or three seats to stretch over on a long flight;

TABLE XIII

NORTH ATLANTIC 'COMPETITION', 1958, 1967 and 1969

	1958			1967			1969		
	Rank	Market Share	Load Factor	Rank	Market Share	Load Factor	Rank	Market Share	Load Facto.
TWA	2	15.2 ⎫	58	2	19.41 ⎫	54	1	21.61 ⎫	52
Pan Am	1	26.3 ⎬ 52.9	63	1	22.72 ⎬ 51.5	56	2	21.20 ⎬ 51.6	53
BOAC	3	11.4 ⎭	68	3	9.42 ⎭	66	3	8.83 ⎭	59
Lufthansa	8	5.2	64	4	8.12	51	4	7.40	52
Air France	5	8.6	64	5	7.76	52	5	7.22	48
Alitalia	10	2.5	53	7	5.30	52	6	5.22	54
SAS	4	9.8	62	8	5.08	57	7	4.77	50
KLM	6	7.4	57	6	5.30	62	8	4.61	55
Irish	13	0.9	37	10	3.63	70	9	3.66	62
Swissair	9	3.9	65	9	3.81	60	10	3.59	51
El Al	11	1.8	59	11	2.44	62	11	2.99	66
Iberia	12	1.0	38	14	1.40	53	12	2.35	46
Sabena	7	5.6	54	12	2.39	60	13	2.09	48
Olympic	—	—	—	13	1.50	51	14	1.65	50
Air India	—	—	—	15	0.97	49	15	0.90	50
TAP	—	—	—	—	—	—	16	0.75	35
Qantas	14	0.5	44	16	0.60	63	17	0.54	58
JAL	—	—	—	17	0.15	30	18	0.35	27
Finnair	—	—	—	—	—	—	19	0.27	34
Average	—	—	61	—	—	56	—	—	53

Sources: IATA unpublished. We should like to thank *Flight International* for the above information originally provided by IATA.

(7) quality of the food—even within the restrictions imposed by IATA rules some airlines manage to create a reputation for good (and for bad) food;[1]

(8) prejudice—probably the bias against non-European pilots is countered by the prejudice for non-European air hostesses;

(9) general courtesy and a willingness to issue free food tickets promptly on learning of a delay;

(10) advertising—most of which seeks to highlight *or* overcome points 1–9.

Given that it is difficult and highly subjective to evaluate any of the above factors it is not surprising to find that, despite five new entrants to the market over the period 1958 to 1969, there has been little change in the 'competitive' position. The top three airlines remain identical, as indeed does the make-up of the leading 10 airlines. As in the world market, Lufthansa, Irish and Alitalia are the successes, climbing four places each in the market table. Pan Am has lost the lead to TWA. The new concerns have made little or no ground and, with the exception of Air India and Olympic, have extremely poor load factors.

During the first six months of 1970 the market grew 23.5 per cent, the most notable feature being that BOAC has been overtaken by Lufthansa and Air France in market share. BOAC has been conducting a stand-still operation which has resulted in a 59.1 per cent load factor (second only to El Al with 68 per cent) but only in a 2.2 per cent growth. The principal reason for this move is not that (at least in the short run) it is good economics but rather that the Americans have increased capacity considerably (which has been accompanied by hints from the Board of Trade about cutting back their frequency), and that BOAC's 747s have remained grounded due to the dispute with their pilots. BOAC's view is that it achieves high load-factors because of the attraction of the VC10. An equally plausible hypothesis is that high load-factors are necessary to cover the relatively higher operating costs of the VC10 compared with the 707.

The entry of new airlines to the market adds little or nothing to consumer choice but simply to total capacity, contributing

[1] Swissair certainly has a 'good food' rating.

to extra costs and the general lowering of load-factors which dropped from 61 per cent in 1958 to 53 per cent in 1969. Indeed, the degree of concentration in the market as measured by the top three has remained virtually unchanged at just over half the total market, so it cannot be claimed that the new airlines added proportionately more custom to the rapidly growing market. Between 1958 and 1967 the number of passengers carried increased by 309 per cent but the number of seats available increased by 338 per cent. Table XIV illustrates the highly fluctuating growth rate.

TABLE XIV

ANNUAL GROWTH OF SCHEDULED AIRWAYS:
NORTH ATLANTIC TRAFFIC, 1948–69
(Passengers carried)
per cent

1948	21	1956	21	1964	25
1949	8	1957	22	1965	15
1950	16	1958	27	1966	15
1951	8	1959	19	1967	17
1952	31	1960	25	1968	5
1953	17	1961	13	1969	18
1954	11	1962	19		
1955	19	1963	10		

Source: IATA, *World Air Transport Statistics*, 1969.

Charter business has in the past fluctuated around 10 per cent of the IATA traffic, although it is possibly not large enough to have had a significantly depressing effect upon fares. Charter business is currently growing at a higher rate than the scheduled traffic (87 per cent in 1969) and is now at least 25 per cent of the total traffic carried. If the IATA claims are accurate the growth potential is considerable without even adding to the market, for according to IATA three-quarters of the North Atlantic traffic is made up of 'pleasure trips'. Caledonian, one of 15 charter companies on the route, for example, reported their 1970 charter business to be 40 per cent up on 1969. No doubt the 1971 increase in IATA fares will give a further impetus to their trade. But even at £60 return it is still an expensive holiday for most of the British tourist market.

If fares were allowed to vary, a high load-factor would not necessarily be efficient. There would undoubtedly be a public

[42]

willing to pay a fare reflecting the higher costs per seat in order to reap the additional comfort. Indeed Swissair claim that any load-factor over 60 per cent can only detract from an airline's service as the risk of over-booking (necessary due to the regular percentage of people booking but not reporting for a particular flight), resulting in passenger frustration and the lack of last-minute seat availability become major problems. Unfortunately for this argument there exists no evidence that a sizeable part of the market would not prefer to exchange these options for the lower fares associated with better utilisation of capacity.

Airlines coming to the fare tariff conference with load-factors varying from 27 to 68 per cent inevitably have very different cost conditions in mind when adding their vote to a unanimous pricing decision. No doubt new entrants are prepared to operate at low load-factors and sustain losses in order to gain a foothold in the market. Unfortunately the carrot is frequently not economic but national prestige. Not even the efficient and market-leading airlines are today finding the North Atlantic route remunerative.

IATA's response to falling load-factors is perversely to raise fares. Load-factors are, however, not exclusively related to demand. They depend not only upon the demand for crossing the Atlantic but also upon the number of planes provided to serve it. Falling load-factors reflect excess capacity—the cure for which is scarcely to raise fares. Commenting on a net overall profit of 0.4 per cent of revenue in 1968, Sir Anthony Milward (BEA) remarked:

'Small wonder that the industry is in such difficulties and will continue to be unless the general public is able to face up to higher charges'.[1]

But the way to fill seats is to lower not raise fares. The only way to fill the 747 is to extend the market or reduce the number of airlines and/or planes in the air. Raising fares will neither (a) increase the total size of the market (although of course it *may* increase total revenue depending upon the elasticity of demand), nor (b) reduce capacity. Raising fares simply reduces the economic pressures on the small and inefficient airlines and, if anything, encourages new capacity in the form of new entrants or of new airlines putting 747s into the air.

[1] Sir Anthony Millward quoted in the *Guardian*, 7 December, 1970.

[43]

There are already 80 747s in current operation and a further 120 on order (at £8.3 million each). Add to these 117 Lockheed Ten-11s and 240 DC-10s and there will be 50 per cent more capacity than already available. Admittedly the 747s are said by Pan Am to have a modest break-even load-factor of 45–50 per cent. Nevertheless a formidable capacity problem is on the horizon. The bewildered public faces the prospect of being told on the one hand that 747s will reduce costs and on the other that they must face higher fares to pay for them. Pan Am's experience with 747s in 1970 indicates that they are 32 per cent cheaper to fly than 707s per passenger-seat available. But whilst early in 1970 they achieved a 59 per cent load factor on the New York–London run, by the last quarter it had fallen to 40 per cent. The airline, faced with a predicted growth of traffic in 1971 of only 2–5 per cent, has been laying off some 5 per cent of its staff. 'There is just too much equipment around,' a spokesman said.[1]

Charter, ITX and excursion fares have clearly shown that a ready market exists at the right level. It may be that, at trans-atlantic fares of £104–20 return, demand may be inelastic (i.e., a small fare increase may produce an increase in total revenue), but that is not to say that a large price reduction could not have a far higher revenue response. Such a move, however, would send some small high-cost airlines to the wall (or at least ought to), which the IATA cartel exists precisely to prevent.

The possible addition of the new Caledonian-BUA line to the North Atlantic lists is an interesting extension of current muddled thinking. This line is to 'add to competition', it is claimed. But as it will be compelled to charge the same fares, provide the same width of seat, the same type of food, etc., in what sense will it add anything except still more excess capacity? It will simply spread the same market out a little thinner, without significant addition to consumer choice, although it may demonstrate that private airlines can operate at lower costs than public airlines.

(iii) *Bilateralism*

Routes are not typically like the North Atlantic. The pattern of 'competition' between any two centres is set not by IATA

---

[1] Quoted in the *Guardian*, 7 January, 1971.

but by the bilateral agreement between two governments. Typically this procedure results in the licensing of two airlines, one from each of the two nation-states. Agreements between them range from the frequency of flights to a complete pooling of revenue. The costs of the two lines involved may be widely different; so there will be pressure to cover the higher of the two cost curves. These two airlines, although subject to the agreement of their IATA colleagues at the conference table (even if other lines do not serve the points, they have a vested interest in seeing that the fare per kilometre-ton is not too obviously less than their own rates on adjacent and possibly substitute routes), will of necessity collude to arrive at a common price. There is no reason why the lowest possible rational price should ever reach the tariff book. The extremes within which agreement must be reached will be the more efficient company's and the inefficient company's profit maximising prices. The outcome is anybody's guess. The issue will be further complicated by the two airlines' respective total market power and the importance of a particular route to their total trading positions. The only certain result of this situation is that the consumer will be ill-served. If the revenue is pooled the two lines may seek to maximise their joint profits, although this is unlikely as it implies agreeing to a common cost curve. Indeed the final outcome is likely to reflect neither party's cost conditions but an administrative and political compromise.

Inefficient high-cost airlines backed by protective governments are not only subsidised by their own nationals' tax payments but also by consumers the world over. Every time a British subject boards a plane bound for given destinations he effectively contributes to keeping the inefficient airlines in the air whether he flies with them or not. He is forced to pay a fare in excess of that possible from a free market BEA or BOAC.

VI. THE INSTITUTIONAL FRAMEWORK

(i) *Safety*

The issue of safety is a large red herring. Price competition, it is argued, would lead to corner-cutting and endanger the public. There is no reason to suppose that corner-cutting to save costs when faced with *fixed prices* is any the less likely. If costs are above the IATA price, or profits are dwindling, exactly the same motive for criminal folly exists. There is no substitute for regulation and inspection under any system. The main safeguard will remain that a bad safety record results in no-one flying with the airline in question (or, more to the point, no-one being willing to fly the planes).

(ii) *Infra-structure*

The infra-structure of airports and connections with city-centres is a huge and rapidly increasing problem. It is taking less and less time to travel and more and more time to arrive. The time spent on the ground is now typically 30 per cent of the total travelling time from London to New York, centre to centre. The main issue is not only how to speed up and make more efficient getting to the airport and boarding the plane but also who should pay. Is it equitable that the 10 per cent who fly should be subsidised by the 90 per cent who do not but who pay taxes and often have to put up with the noise of take-offs and landings?

(iii) *Cracks in the tariff structure*

In recent months both BEA and BOAC have begun to show concern with the IATA tariff structure. BOAC have pioneered the 'Early Bird' system which enables them to tap a share of the charter market and remain free of the 'affinity group' and ITX restrictions. Passengers prepared to book four months in advance of flying, to make a non-returnable deposit and to accept a variable departure date have been offered sizeable reductions in the IATA tariff. This offer is at present restricted to trips to Bermuda and Antigua and is available only to the citizens of the Caribbean and the UK. The length of stay is also restricted to the 14–60 day return period. The fare to Bermuda is exactly halved and that to Antigua reduced by about 45 per cent.

BOAC have for some time repeatedly made attempts to extend the 'Early Bird' principle. In October 1969 they attempted to get an £83 return flight to New York accepted by rival IATA lines but without success. Indeed the desired fare was earlier rumoured to be £65 return. Again they asked IATA for a 50 per cent reduction on the London–Australia route but the Australians are known to favour high fares and strict frequency controls.[1] An attempt to block American airlines from serving Sydney was recently made but failed when the US threatened to withdraw from Qantas rights to cross the USA. BOAC are, however, shortly adding St Lucia to their list and are to apply to IATA and the government once more for extensions of the service—this time to Jamaica, Barbados and Trinidad.

The other development is that BEA have managed to get limited freedom to charge 'charter level' rates to ITX tour and the government operators on some routes. Tour operators need take only 10 seats on any given scheduled flight instead of, as formerly, charter a whole plane to avoid ITX fare restrictions (i.e., normally that the package tour price should not be lower than the IATA return fare). There is also every indication that BEA is attempting to increase its share of charter traffic through its subsidiary Airtours, which is charging very low rates, possibly cross-subsidised from the scheduled traffic revenue of the parent company. These developments are attempts to fill surplus capacity. Concern is widespread that capacity has increased 240 per cent over the past 10 years but passengers only 200 per cent.

These relaxations in fare structure are a reaction to empty seats on holiday routes competing directly with charter services. Unfortunately they are a reaction, not an initiative in expanding consumer choice and creating new markets. They are welcome nonetheless.

(iv) *IATA attempts to counter charter competition*

IATA concern over charter competition is currently at a new peak. Accusations are being made by scheduled airline chiefs that the non-scheduled airlines take traffic away from rather than add to the total market. Mr I. Bruno Velani, President of Alitalia, considered that their 'dangerous activities' should be restricted by quotas. In the summer of 1969, he said, charter companies took 39 per cent of the New York–Rome traffic, 67 per cent of New York–Amsterdam, and 68 per cent of New York–Frankfurt. Mr Hammarskjold saw them as responsible

---

[1] They also in effect bar charter flights. The only non-scheduled airline charter service to Australia consists of a charter flight to Singapore followed by a transfer to a scheduled airline.

for the present over-capacity in the industry but was met by the retort from Peter Hodgens (Council of Europe) that

'I don't believe one can cut off the development of mass holiday traffic in order to keep scheduled airlines marginally solvent.'[1]

SAS has recently reported that it was responding to charter competition by developing its own non-scheduled services at a faster rate.[2]

Ironically, BEA (at the forefront of the move to reduce restrictions on ITX fares) has recently but unsuccessfully opposed a licence for Dan Air to fly Lunn Poly long weekend holidays to Stockholm, Vienna and Rome for £25, on the ground that such trips would divert traffic from scheduled flights.[3]

Nor has chartering by IATA members themselves escaped criticism. The IATA 'task force' has uncovered over 40 breaches of the affinity rules amongst its own members. Mr Hammarskjold in a characteristic speech said of them:

'When they are caught, some are even covered up by their own authorities. This state of affairs seems to be becausethey are airlines which have overstretched themselves and can only remain in the market through the use of clearly uneconomical and unethical business practices'.[4]

They may be 'unethical' but it is hard to see why they should do it if they are also uneconomic.

The small national airlines not surprisingly have been pressing for more co-operation and generally expressing dissatisfaction with the extension of promotional fares. One said at the IATA General Meeting in Teheran in 1970, 'the basic trouble was the atomistic outlook of individual carriers'. The host-country's Prime Minister regretted that airlines sometimes overlooked the necessity for 'such international co-operation as was necessary for fair and equal sharing of advantages and

[1] Symposium on Tourism and Air Transport, Institut du Transport Aerien (ITA), reported in *Flight International*, 10 December, 1970.
[2] *Flight International*, 3 December, 1970.
[3] *Flight International*, 1 October, 1970.
[4] K. Hammarskjold, address to the Annual General Meeting of IATA, Teheran, 1970, reported in *The Times*, 27 October, 1970.

a full appreciation of all parties' rights'. The outgoing President at the meeting referred to the

'excess dilution of revenue yields from promotional fares', and added: 'We may have to ask ourselves whether our present processes for reaching agreement are still adequate'.[1]

Indeed it has been proposed that the unanimity voting rule should be changed to one of an 80 per cent majority, but the American Civil Aeronautics Board has made it clear that it would oppose any such move.

VII. PROPOSALS FOR REFORM: MASS AIR TRAVEL WITH CHOICE?

If any good *economic* reasons for not having 'freedom of the air' have been deduced, they are yet to appear in print. The argument that a free market in passenger services would result in chaos with rate 'wars' and bewildered uninformed consumers swamped with conflicting information is not convincing. Air transport is a highly concentrated industry with only some 100 companies of all sizes operating in a market which has formidable natural entry barriers to protect it: a new international airline would have to face enormous initial investment in equipment, the training of personnel and world-wide promotion. Concern would be directed not so much towards the danger of too much competition but rather towards too little—and the need for anti-trust legislation. In a market which naturally disaggregates into a series of route sub-markets, all oligopolistic, fares would be sticky and price leadership (tacit or explicit) common. Airlines would be more likely to compete with product differentiation than with price once fares had found a market level.[2]

The only argument against freeing civil aviation from all but safety controls is that it is *politically* unlikely to gain universal support. Many politicians regard their airlines as flag ships representing their country abroad. Thus the planes must be modern, the sales offices lavish, the uniforms grand, and the plane markings seen in as many of the world's airports as frequently as possible.

[1] *The Times*, 27 October, 1970.
[2] B. S. Yamey, *Resale Price Maintenance*, Hobart Paper No. 1, Institute of Economic Affairs, London, 1959.

Reform by governments: regulated competition?

Reform is the province of governments alone.[1] By their control of the right to land they hold all the bargaining power and strength. They have in any case two direct stakes in the industry. In all countries they subsidise the industry either directly or by supporting the infra-structure. They also have a considerable direct share-holding. Thirteen of Europe's airlines are 100 per cent state-owned, a further 11 state-controlled, four jointly-owned, and five have some state holding. Only nine are completely independent. Outside Europe at least 20 major airlines are completely state-owned and a further 24 state-controlled.

The present structure has little or nothing to recommend it save that it gives governments and airline chiefs a quiet life. Consumers in the Western world, however, are beginning to realise that they are paying too high a price for somebody else's peace of mind. There are basically two directions for reform to take. The first is amalgamation and rationalisation.[2] The number of airlines in the world could be drastically reduced (conceivably to one) and civil aviation run by the ICAO as a 'public service' receiving world-wide subsidisation. Nation-states would subsidise such an organisation out of tax funds in direct proportion to their nationals' share of passenger-miles. Civil aviation would become a politically co-operative venture. Such a reform, however, is unlikely to serve consumer interest any better than the *status quo*.

The second, and to us desirable, approach is to introduce regulated competition in some economically meaningful sense. This implies freedom to vary fares and quality of provision. It also implies explicit subsidies to keep unprofitable services and airlines in the air for prestige, defence, social benefits and any other reason thought proper by any nation. The costs of these

---

[1] Reform is not promised by the latest White Paper (*Civil Aviation Policy*, Cmnd. 4213, HMSO, November 1969) or by the Civil Aviation Bill. Both these documents accept the *status quo* arguing that it is 'an inescapable fact that international services depend upon a network of agreements with other countries defining traffic rights which airlines may employ'. To accept this is to preserve IATA and to believe, as did the Edward Committee (*op. cit.*,) that an alternative institutional framework ought not to be beyond the wit of man and could benefit all parties concerned, including consumers.

[2] A small degree of rationalisation has taken place. KLM, Swissair, SAS and UTA have formed themselves into a group, as have Air France, Alitalia, Lufthansa, Sabena and Iberia, to facilitate joint maintenance and equipment purchases. Since the time of writing rumours of mergers between US carriers have been rife in the face of the large losses expected in 1971.

subsidies should fall exclusively on the tax-payers voting for the services and not on the consumers of other states.

Licensing by public tender

A world licensing body of Government representatives (possibly ICAO) would agree to license companies to fly stated routes for a minimum but renewable period of, say, five years. The number licensed on any route could be open to negotiation but in no case would it be less than three with the two nations linked by the route guaranteed one licence each.

All licences apart from the two guaranteed would be allocated on the basis of public tenders. Airlines would be invited to tender for given classes of traffic and of booking conditions. A maximum fare for any given class of service equal to the highest accepted tender fare would be imposed on the route. The lowest tenders for, say, three distinct classes of traffic would be awarded contracts subject to cancellation for

(1) attempting to raise fares;

(2) changing conditions of booking;

(3) serious quality deterioration;

(4) any safety infringement.

Competition would come from two sources: first, the other licensed carriers and, secondly, the fear of losing the licence at the end of five years. All carriers would be free to *reduce* fares at any time.[1] For its part the licensing body would be free to impose

(1) minimum and/or maximum frequency conditions;

(2) safety standards and inspection; and

(3) upon the request of any individual government, enforced but fully subsidised 'public service' flights. These would be paid for *via* the licensing authority by the requesting nation or nations.

Although the proposal appears complex it is at the very least simpler than the present Government/IATA complex,

[1] It has been argued that as many airlines are state-owned price competition is impractical as some States would pour subsidies into their flag carriers (much as France did before and after the war) and hence compete 'unfairly'. If they did this, the nationals of other countries would enjoy 'free rides'. So long as the prices were forced down to competitive levels, why worry?

and allows for competition within a regulated framework and for prestige carriers on all routes. Further the subsidy to keep inefficient prestige lines in the air falls where it belongs—on the nationals enjoying the prestige.

The main opposition to such a scheme can be expected to come from the smaller prestige airlines and the inefficient. The governments that control landing rights in the world's key airports must be the final arbitrators. The existing system is in large part the outcome of compromise between Britain and the USA, and it is probably to these countries that we must turn for the first steps towards reform.

VIII. SUMMARY AND CONCLUSIONS

The conclusions reached in this analysis may be set out in a series of findings.

1. Civil aviation is, despite a 14 per cent per annum growth in passenger-miles flown, an infant industry with enormous scope for expansion.

2. The present structure of the industry is largely the result of a compromise in 1946 between politicians or governments desiring 'freedom in the air' analogous to that in shipping, and those determined to maintain sovereignty over their airspace and control the right of other parties to land.

3. Governments by default ceded all tariff matters to the airlines themselves to determine within a producers' cartel (IATA).

4. Whilst governments have retained the power to veto fares agreed within IATA, in practice they have rarely employed it.

5. The cartel has, besides enforcing uniform tariffs on all members, restricted competition in quality. This inhibition has not prevented high advertising and selling outlays spent in the attempt to differentiate the otherwise largely homogeneous products.

6. The cartel has been open-ended with the result that it has both protected current capacity and encouraged still more. Fares have been maintained at artificially high levels in an attempt to cover inflated costs. The result has been that much market potential remains unexploited.

[52]

7. There are wide variations in load-factors and therefore costs per mile flown between airlines. They are reflected in large variations in scheduled fares per mile.

8. Excess capacity has kept profits extremely low; with the introduction of 747s they continue to deteriorate.

9. IATA has reacted to excess capacity by raising rather than lowering fares.

10. The industry is highly concentrated with stable market shares. Only the North Atlantic has a significant number of airlines serving it. Most routes are subject to bilateral agreement between governments.

11. What little competition now exists springs from the charter companies outside IATA. The impact of this competition has been hindered by affinity and other rules. They are not in the public interest and should be abolished.

12. Scheduled airlines have introduced promotional fares as a reaction to charter competition rather than as an initiative in tapping new markets.

13. The present system is found to be against the consumers' best interests.

14. Price competition within a system of international licensing regulation strictly confined to safety is proposed.

The principal ill in the current civil aviation industry is that airlines are deciding what is good for the passenger. Technical 'progress' is made with little if any consideration of the demand for it. National governments eager for 'prestige' lines and airlines eager for 'prestige' planes have both come to expect the consumer to pay to keep both in the air. Excess capacity pervades the industry and the consumer is expected to pay for empty seats he has not asked for.

The normal sanction of going out of business does not exist, nor the carrot of profits. Only by allowing airlines to vary their product mix freely and to reflect it in their fare structures can mass air travel become a reality. At present there is neither a rational 'public service' industry nor consumer sovereignty and choice in a competitive market. Reform is long overdue.

SUGGESTED QUESTIONS FOR DISCUSSION

1. In what ways is the IATA cartel worse for the public than would be an outright monopoly of the industry by a single firm?

2. In the absence of IATA, technological progress might be introduced at a slower rate. What effect would slower innovation have on the public interest?

3. Why, in the absence of IATA, would the entry of new airlines be more, rather than less, difficult?

4. Given that IATA is a 'price maker', why are there no excess profits in the industry?

5. What are the main characteristics of an industry that determine whether a large or small number of firms is most beneficial to the public interest?

6. Does the concept of elasticity of demand help to explain why a group on holiday can fly to New York for 2.5 (old) pence per mile but a businessman for 6.1 (old) pence?

7. Which airlines are likely to resist the introduction of a licensing system as proposed in the text?

8. How might the governments of nations with large and relatively efficient airlines induce the small countries to accept a more liberal licensing framework for civil aviation?

9. In what ways have the scheduled airlines been inconsistent in their opposition to charter competition?

10. How will the eventual availability of supersonic aircraft affect the analysis and conclusions of this *Paper?*

FURTHER READING

Bach, G. L., *Economics*, 6th edition, Prentice-Hall, 1968.

Straszheim, M. R. *The International Airline Industry*, The Brookings Institution, Washington, 1969.

Rosenberg, A., *Air Travel Within Europe*, Swedish Consumer Council, Stockholm, 1970.

Pillai, K. G. J., *The Air Net*, Grossman Publishers, New York, 1969.

Wheatcroft, S., *The Economics of European Air Transport*, Manchester University Press, 1956.

— *Air Transport Policy*, Michael Joseph, London, 1964.

Brooks, P. W., 'The Development of Air Transport', *Journal of Transport Economics and Policy*, 1967.

Civil Aviation Policy, Cmnd. 4213, HMSO, November 1969.

Seekings, J., *Guidlines for Airlines*, CPC, London, 1970.

British Air Transport in the Seventies—The Edwards Committee Report, The UK Committee of Inquiry into Civil Air Transport, Cmnd. 4018, HMSO, May 1969.

[55]

IEA SUBSCRIPTION SERVICE

An annual subscription to the IEA ensures that all regular series, research studies, etc., are sent without further charge immediately on publication—representing a substantial saving.

The cost (including postage is £5.25 for twelve months (£5 by Banker's Order); £6.30 or $15 for overseas subscriptions.